S0-CUF-172

Jan 1 1970

To
my Grandson
Gus Niebuhr

May the study
of these lines bring
comfort to thy heart
in this changing world.
And may we hope
for a life for mankind
that embraces all good
in the past two thousand
years and reject all
bad in years to come!

Grandad
N S Mulhearn

# A TIME FOR PEACE

## Verses from the Bible

Selected, edited, and with an introduction by

Louis Untermeyer

Illustrated by Joan Berg Victor

The World Publishing Company

New York and Cleveland

In all cases, the verses in this book were selected from the King James Bible, although in some cases the entire verse has not been included.



Published by the World Publishing Company
110 East 59th Street, New York, New York 10022
Published simultaneously in Canada by
Nelson, Foster & Scott Ltd.
Library of Congress catalog card number: 70-82780
 Printed in the United States of America.
Typography by Jack Jaget

# AN INTRODUCTION

In a warring world there have always been protesting voices, voices crying passionately for peace. Such cries, ringing throughout the Bible, speak to us with particular poignancy today. If ever there was a longing for peace, that time is now.

Milton's adage that "peace hath her victories no less renowned than war" is actually an understatement, for the victories achieved in peace mean more to the family of man than all the triumphs of war. It is in peace that swords can be beaten into plowshares and spears into pruning hooks, that factories geared to produce engines of destruction can turn to building better communities and better lives, that scientists can find ways of replenishing the land instead of devastating it.

The poets have always known this. They have echoed the Psalms that declare we must "seek peace and ensue it," that we must "heed the thing that is right, for that shall bring a man peace at the last." Shakespeare's Cardinal Wolsey, ruined by a lust for power, found comfort in the thought of a peace "which passeth all understanding," a peace "above all earthly dignities."

Love thyself last: cherish those hearts that hate thee;
Corruption wins not more than honesty.
Still in thy right hand carry gentle peace . . .

Isaiah prophesied the coming of one who, having every attribute of glory, "shall be called Wonderful, Counsellor, the mighty God, the everlasting Father," and who would bring the greatest blessing of all, "The Prince of Peace." Tennyson had this hope in mind when, in "The Golden Year," he longed for the time when all men's good

> Be each man's rule, and univeral peace
> Lie like a shaft of light across the land . . .

Tennyson said it again, with greater challenge, in *In Memoriam:*

> Ring out old shapes of foul disease;
>    Ring out the narrowing lust of gold;
>    Ring out the thousand wars of old;
> Ring in the thousand years of peace.

That pure visionary, William Blake, could see a world in a grain of sand, a heaven in a wild flower, and eternity in an hour. Blake cried out in "Auguries of Innocence":

> The soldier, arm'd with sword and gun,
> Palsied strikes the summer's sun.
> . . . . . . . . . . . . .
> Nought can deform the human race
> Like to the armour's iron brace.
> When gold and gems adorn the plough
> To peaceful arts shall Envy bow.

It was also Blake who invoked the fulfillment of mankind's deepest and most urgent desires in eight lines of "The Divine Image":

To Mercy, Pity, Peace, and Love
All pray in their distress:
And to these virtues of delight
Return their thankfulness.

. . . . . . . . . . . . . .

For Mercy has a human heart;
Pity a human face;
And Love, the human form divine;
And Peace the human dress.

A hundred years after Blake, A. E. Housman grieved over the injustices, the desperate endeavors, and the threats of lawless death which plague mankind. He, too, found consolation in the "ensured release" which peace brings to all. He said it in the last poem of his last book.

Good night; ensured release,
Imperishable peace,
Have these for yours,
While sea abides, and land,
And earth's foundations stand,
And heaven endures.

Nowhere has the cessation of warfare and the beneficent spread of peace been summoned more suggestively than in a single image which I adapted from a *haiku* by the Japanese poet Basho.

On the mouth of a
Cannon half-buried in earth
A butterfly sleeps.

Today, more than ever, we know, as Benjamin Franklin assured us, "there never was a good war or a bad peace." Times and conditions have changed with the centuries, but hatred still persists. Violence has taken on more terrifying forms with every decade. The world, torn apart by disruptive passions and equipped with incalculable means of destruction, may well annihilate itself. We are faced with ultimates; our choice is not between alternations of wars and temporary cease-fires but between world desolation and world peace.

Can a peaceful world ever be achieved? To gain universal peace can the hearts of men be changed? There are those who have always believed that the human race can—and must—be changed for the better. It is not only the saints and prophets, the idealists, the persuaders and believers in human perfectibility, who have imagined it, but also the countless inarticulate millions who have hoped for it and who are at one in spirit, if not in action, with the young people who, clamoring for an end of bloodshed, carry placards proclaiming "Make love, not war."

The passages from the Bible which have been chosen for this book illuminate every page. Strongly and joyously they affirm the faith that care and kindness can take the place of killing, that unity and concord can be established between nations as well as between individuals, that the light still shines in darkness, and that the peace which was promised and so often deferred can, with hearts that are dedicated and minds that are determined, finally be fulfilled.

LOUIS UNTERMEYER

# A TIME FOR PEACE

And suddenly there was the angel
A multitude of the heavenly host
Praising God, and saying,
Glory to God in the highest
And on earth peace,
Good will toward men.

LUKE 2:13–14

Ho, every one that thirsteth, come ye to the waters,
And he that hath no money; come ye, buy, and eat;
Yea, come, buy wine and milk without money and without
price.

Wherefore do ye spend money for that which is not bread?
And your labour for that which satisfieth not?
Hearken diligently unto me, and eat ye that which is good,
And let your soul delight itself in fatness.

Incline your ear, and come unto me:
Hear, and your soul shall live;
And I will make an everlasting covenant with you,
Even the sure mercies of David.

Behold, I have given him for a witness to the people,
A leader and commander to the people.

Behold, thou shalt call a nation that thou knowest not,
And nations that knew not thee shall run unto thee because
Of the Lord thy God, and for the Holy One of Israel;
For he hath glorified thee.

Seek ye the Lord while he may be found,
Call ye upon him while he is near:
Let the wicked forsake his way,

And the unrighteous man his thoughts:
And let him return unto the Lord,
And he will have mercy upon him;
And to our God, for he will abundantly pardon.

For my thoughts are not your thoughts,
Neither are your ways my ways, saith the Lord.
For as the heavens are higher than the earth,
So are my ways higher than your ways,
And my thoughts than your thoughts.

For as the rain cometh down, and the snow from heaven,
And returneth not thither, but watereth the earth,
And maketh it bring forth and bud
That it may give seed to the sower, and bread to the eater:
So shall my word be that goeth forth out of my mouth:
It shall not return unto me void,
But it shall accomplish that which I please,
And it shall prosper in the thing whereto I sent it.

For ye shall go out with joy, and be led forth with peace:
The mountains and the hills shall break forth before you into singing,
And all the trees of the field shall clap their hands.

ISAIAH 55:1–12

Then shall the lame man leap as an hart,
And the tongue of the dumb sing:
For in the wilderness shall waters break out, and streams
in the desert.

And the parched ground shall become a pool,
And the thirsty land springs of water:
In the habitation of dragons, where each lay, shall be grass
with reeds and rushes.

And an highway shall be there, and a way,
And it shall be called The way of holiness;
The unclean shall not pass over it;
But it shall be for those:
The wayfaring men, though fools, shall not err therein.

No lion shall be there,
Nor any ravenous beast shall go up thereon,
It shall not be found there;
But the redeemed shall walk there:
And the ransomed of the Lord shall return,
And come to Zion with songs and everlasting joy upon
their heads:
They shall obtain joy and gladness,
And sorrow and sighing shall flee away.

ISAIAH 35:6–10

The wolf also shall dwell with the lamb,
And the leopard shall lie down with the kid;
And the calf and the young lion and the fatling together;
And a little child shall lead them.

And the cow and the bear shall feed;
Their young ones shall lie down together;
And the lion shall eat straw like the ox.

ISAIAH 11:6–7

Behold, the Lord God will come with a strong hand, and his arm shall rule for him: behold, his reward is with him, and his work before him.

He shall feed his flock like a shepherd: he shall gather the lambs with his arm, and carry them in his bosom, and shall gently lead those that are with young.

Who hath measured the waters in the hollow of his hand, and meted out heaven with the span, and comprehended the dust of the earth in a measure, and weighed the mountains in scales, and the hills in a balance?

Who hath directed the Spirit of the Lord, or being his counsellor hath taught him?

With whom took he counsel, and who instructed him, and taught him in the path of judgment, and taught him knowledge, and shewed to him the way of understanding?

Behold, the nations are as a drop of a bucket, and are counted as the small dust of the balance: behold he taketh up the isles as a very little thing.

ISAIAH 40:10–15

To every thing there is a season,
And a time to every purpose under the heaven:
A time to be born, and a time to die;
A time to plant, and a time to pluck up that which is
planted;
A time to kill, and a time to heal;
A time to break down, and a time to build up;
A time to weep, and a time to laugh;
A time to mourn, and a time to dance;
A time to cast away stones, and a time to gather stones
together;
A time to embrace, and a time to refrain from embracing;
A time to get, and a time to lose;
A time to keep, and a time to cast away;
A time to rend, and a time to sew;
A time to keep silence, and a time to speak;
A time to love, and a time to hate;
A time of war, and a time of peace.

ECCLESIASTES 3:1–8

What doth it profit, my brethren, though a man say he hath faith, and have not works? Can faith save him?

If a brother or sister be naked, and destitute of daily food, and one of you say unto them, Depart in peace, be ye warmed and filled; notwithstanding ye give them not those things which are needful to the body. What doth it profit?

Even so faith, if it hath not works, is dead, being alone.

JAMES 2:14–17

But the wisdom that is from above is first pure, then peaceable, gentle, and easy to be intreated, full of mercy and good fruits, without partiality, and without hypocrisy.

And the fruit of righteousness is sown in peace of them that make peace.

JAMES 3:17–18

The harvest truly is great, but the labourers are few:
Pray ye therefore the Lord of the harvest,
That he would send forth labourers into his harvest.

Go your ways: behold, I send you forth as lambs among wolves.
Carry neither purse, nor scrip, nor shoes:
And salute no man by the way.
And into whatsoever house ye enter,
First say, Peace be to this house.

LUKE 10:2–5

Thou hast put gladness in my heart, more than in the time that their corn and their wine increased.

I will both lay me down in peace, and sleep: for thou, Lord, only makest me dwell in safety.

PSALMS 4:7–8

He hath blessed thy children within thee.
He maketh peace in thy borders
And filleth thee with the finest of the wheat.

PSALMS 147:13–14

For a small moment have I forsaken thee; but with great mercies will I gather thee.

In a little wrath I hid my face from thee for a moment; but with everlasting kindness will I have mercy on thee, saith the Lord thy Redeemer.

For this is as the waters of Noah unto me: for as I have sworn that the waters of Noah should no more go over the earth; so have I sworn that I would not be wroth with thee, nor rebuke thee.

For the mountains shall depart, and the hills be removed; but my kindness shall not depart from thee, neither shall the covenant of my peace be removed, saith the Lord that hath mercy on thee.

O thou afflicted, tossed with tempest, and not comforted, behold, I will lay thy stones with fair colours, and lay thy foundations with sapphires.

And I will make thy windows of agates, and thy gates of carbuncles, and all thy borders of pleasant stones.

And all thy children shall be taught of the Lord; and great shall be the peace of thy children.

ISAIAH 54:7–13

Build ye houses, and dwell in them; and plant gardens and eat the fruit of them;

Take ye wives, and beget sons and daughters; and take wives for your sons, and give your daughters to husbands, that they may bear sons and daughters; that ye may be increased there, and not diminished.

And seek the peace of the city whither I have caused you to be carried away captives, and pray unto the Lord for it: for in the peace thereof shall ye have peace.

JEREMIAH 29:5–7

For I know the thoughts that I think toward you, saith the Lord, thoughts of peace and not of evil, to give you an expected end.

Then shall ye call upon me, and ye shall go and pray unto me, and I will hearken unto you.

And ye shall seek me, and find me, when ye shall search for me with all your heart.

JEREMIAH 29:11–13

And the city had no need of the sun, neither of the moon, to shine in it: for the glory of God did lighten it, and the Lamb is the light thereof.

And the nations of them which are saved shall walk in the light of it: and the kings of the earth do bring their glory and honour into it.

And the gates of it shall not be shut at all by day: for there shall be no night there.

And they shall bring the glory and honour of the nations into it.

And there shall in no wise enter into it any thing that defileth, neither whatsoever worketh abomination, or maketh a lie: but they which are written in the Lamb's book of life.

REVELATION 21:23–27

And he shewed me a pure river of water of life, clear as crystal, proceeding out of the throne of God and of the Lamb.

In the midst of the street of it, and on either side of the river, was there the tree of life, which bare twelve manner of fruits, and yielded her fruit every month: and the leaves of the tree were for the healing of the nations.

And there shall be no more curse: but the throne of God and of the Lamb shall be in it; and his servants shall serve him:

And they shall see his face; and his name shall be in their foreheads.

And there shall be no night there; and they need no candle, neither light of the sun; for the Lord God giveth them light: and they shall reign for ever and ever.

And he said unto me, These sayings are faithful and true: and the Lord God of the holy prophets sent his angel to shew unto his servants the things which must shortly be done.

REVELATION 22:1–6

Follow peace with all men, and holiness, without which no man shall see the Lord.

HEBREWS 12:14

Let brotherly love continue.

Be not forgetful to entertain strangers; for thereby some have entertained angels unawares.

HEBREWS 13:1–2

How beautiful upon the mountains are the feet of him that bringeth good tidings, that publisheth peace.

ISAIAH 52:7

If any man have an ear, let him hear.
He that leadeth into captivity shall go into captivity:
He that killeth with the sword must be killed with the
sword.
Here is the patience and the faith of the saints.

REVELATION 13:9–10

For he that will love life, and see good days, let him refrain his tongue from evil, and his lips that they speak no guile: Let him eschew evil, and do good; let him seek peace, and ensue it.

I PETER 3:10–11

Peace, peace to him that is far off, and to him that is near, saith the Lord, and I will heal him.

But the wicked are like the troubled sea, when it cannot rest, whose waters cast up mire and dirt.

There is no peace, saith my God, to the wicked.

ISAIAH 57:19–21

Owe no man anything but to love one another;
for he that loveth another hath fulfilled the law.
Love worketh no ill to his neighbour;
therefore love is the fulfilling of the law.

ROMANS 13:8, 13:10

Peace I leave with you, my peace I give unto you: not as the world giveth, give I unto you. Let not your heart be troubled, neither let it be afraid.

JOHN 14:27

Blessed are the poor in spirit: for theirs is the kingdom of heaven.
Blessed are they that mourn: for they shall be comforted.
Blessed are the meek: for they shall inherit the earth.
Blessed are they which do hunger and thirst after righteousness: for they shall be filled.
Blessed are the merciful: for they shall obtain mercy.
Blessed are the pure in heart: for they shall see God.
Blessed are the peacemakers: for they shall be called the children of God.

MATTHEW 5:3–9

The Lord bless thee, and keep thee:
The Lord make his face shine upon thee, and be gracious unto thee:
The Lord lift up his countenance upon thee, and give thee peace.

NUMBERS 6:24–26

**Louis Untermeyer**, poet, editor, short story writer, and lecturer, has published more than ninety books. He has received the Gold Medal of the Poetry Society of America, and for the years 1961 through 1963 was Consultant in Poetry to the Library of Congress. This is his second book of Bible verse published by The World Publishing Company and illustrated by Joan Berg Victor. The first volume, a collection of Psalms entitled *Songs of Joy*, celebrated the wonder of love and the affirmation of faith.

**Joan Berg Victor** is a painter, draftsman, designer, and book illustrator. She is a graduate of H. Sophie Newcomb College and Yale University Graduate School of Art. Her beautiful pencil drawings and watercolor paintings have enhanced many books, among them a recent picture book for the very young, *Sh-h! Listen Again!*, for which she also wrote the text. Mrs. Victor and her husband and son live in New York City.

1 2 3 4 5 73 72 71 70 69